Copyright

Table of Contents

Disclaimer

This biography, "Fractured Resilience," is based on true events and depicts real individuals and their experiences. However, in order to protect the privacy and identities of the people involved, names, locations, and certain details have been altered or fictionalized.

While every effort has been made to maintain the integrity of the original events and portray the essence of the individuals' stories, it is important to note that the book may not provide a completely accurate or comprehensive account of their lives. Certain events may have been condensed, rearranged, or modified for the purpose of storytelling and to ensure the privacy and confidentiality of the individuals concerned. The author has undertaken diligent research and conducted interviews to present an authentic and heartfelt narrative. However, some dialogues, specific conversations, or internal thoughts may have been reconstructed or reimagined based on the author's understanding and interpretation of the events.

Readers should approach this biography with an understanding that it represents the author's perception and interpretation of the events and the individuals involved. It is not intended as an official or definitive historical record but rather as a personal exploration and tribute to the resilience and strength demonstrated by the individuals in the face of their challenges.

The utmost care has been taken to respect the privacy and well-being of the individuals portrayed in this biography. Any resemblance to other persons, living or deceased, or to real-life events beyond the shared experiences is coincidental. By engaging with this biography, readers acknowledge and understand that while based on real events and individuals, the book may contain elements of creative license and artistic interpretation to enhance the storytelling experience.

It is also not intended to provide medical advice. Readers should consult qualified professionals for personalized advice, as the book may not accurately represent the full scope of mental health conditions. The author and publisher disclaim any liability for reliance on the book's information.

Preface

Dear Readers,

As I sit down to pen these words, I am filled with a mix of trepidation and excitement. The journey that awaits you within the pages of "Fractured Resilience" is one that has been etched deeply into my being—a story that demanded to be told, both for my own healing and to offer solace to those who may find resonance in its words.

This book is a testament to the power of vulnerability, the complexities of the human experience, and the indomitable strength that resides within us all. Through the lens of my own struggles with mental turmoil, legal battles, and the weight of a painful family history, I invite you to explore the depths of the human spirit and psychology and the unyielding capacity for resilience.

Within these chapters, you will bear witness to my journey of self-discovery—a journey that has led me to the darkest corners of my mind, where fears lurk and scars remain. It is an exploration of the shadows we often shy away from, the wounds we try to conceal, and the truths we dare not confront. But amidst the darkness, there is a glimmer of hope, a flicker of resilience that refuses to be extinguished.

"Fractured Resilience" is an invitation to accompany me on a path of redemption, a pilgrimage through the valleys of pain and the peaks of triumph. It is my fervent hope that, through sharing my story, I can inspire you to embrace your own journey, to find solace in knowing that you are not alone, and to discover the strength within you to heal and rise above even the most daunting of obstacles.

I am immensely grateful to you, dear readers, for embarking on this poignant odyssey alongside me. Together, let us navigate the labyrinthine corridors of the human experience, acknowledging both the fractures and the resilience that make us who we are.

With heartfelt gratitude,

Ishani

Beyond the Breaking Point

Attempted Suicide – Take 1

I wake up every morning with the knowledge that I need to kill myself to escape, but a part of me wishes I didn't have to. It's a twisted thought that consumes my every waking moment. I go about my day with a smile on my face, but my mind is always on the ways I could end it all. I've spent countless hours researching the best way to take my own life, but I have to be careful. I don't want anyone to suspect a thing, especially not the insurance company. The last thing I want is for my family to be denied the payout they deserve. It's a strange existence, to be living a life that you know will soon come to an end. I pray for a miracle every second before I need to take my life, but deep down, I know it's unlikely to happen. They say to check in on your happy friends, but who would suspect the happy-go-lucky girl with the infectious laugh is secretly planning her own demise? It's a burden I carry alone, and one that I don't think I can bear for much longer.

November 2021 brought an unexpected event—a gentle snowfall blanketed a nearby town, painting the world in a serene white. It was during this time that I embarked on a trip with my family, a facade of joy masking the tears welling up inside me. Every smile I forced, every picture I took, and every memory I made was a bitter reminder that it would all soon come to an end. I carried my secret burden, seeking solace in prayer, as tears became the only words I could utter. Every song, every movie, every flavor of food, and every breathtaking view—I soaked it all in, desperately clinging to the fleeting moments, aware that they were slipping through my fingers.

A week later, the weight of my pain became unbearable, and I made the decision to take an overdose. I fabricated a story for my parents, telling them I needed to work on some videos and would spend the night in the outbuilding. It wasn't entirely a lie; I did have videos to make. Only, these videos were my farewell, my final message to the world. With a heavy heart, I propped up my phone, pressed record, and mustered the strength to explain why I was about to do what I was about to do. Tears flowed freely as I apologized, as I poured out my emotions, and as I left instructions for my family to navigate the aftermath. In the depths of my soul, I fought against the overwhelming urge to end it all. Part of me longed to be alive, yearned for the heavens to intervene, to send down a miracle that would save me.

I had set a deadline for myself—10 p.m., giving me enough time to slip away into eternal slumber before the morning light. But as the hours ticked away, I found myself unable to take that final step without reaching out to someone, anyone. Determined to break free from the clutches of despair, I picked up the phone and dialed the number of my fiancé. With trembling words, I revealed the truth—the mistakes I had made, the darkness that enveloped me, and my intent to end my own life. It shattered him to his core, leaving him lost and unsure of what to say or do. And at that moment, I broke too. Desperate for a lifeline, I clung to the fragile hope that he could save me. But the weight of the situation was too heavy, and it overwhelmed him as well. After our conversation, after he extracted a promise from me not to go through with it, I took the overdose. There wasn't enough time for it to take the lethal toll, but it was enough to render me semi-unconscious, enough to beg my family to rush me to the hospital.

As I lay in the sterile hospital room, my mother stood by my side, her face etched with worry, while my fiancé tried to come to terms with the magnitude of what had transpired. My sister fought to maintain composure, her strength tested beyond measure, all for the sake of the shattered family we once were. And my father, overwhelmed and shocked, struggled to find his voice amid the storm of emotions.

Attempted Suicide – Take 2

Four months had passed, and on the surface, it seemed as though things had improved. I had been forgiven for my initial mistakes, or so it seemed. But deep within, trapped in a never-ending cycle of guilt and shame, I found myself repeating those same mistakes, and even venturing into darker territory.

This time, I was determined to end my life correctly. I meticulously planned every detail, ensuring the timing was appropriate and that it would work without fail. In my little white book, I wrote an apology for the mistakes I had once again committed. I went a step further, carefully selecting my funeral outfit, leaving everything ready to avoid inconveniencing my family any further. But despite my preparations, my second attempt did not go as planned.

Around 2 a.m., I took the necessary steps to end my life, only to find myself engaged in a fierce internal battle. I didn't want to die. What was I doing? I desperately wanted to undo it. Within the next hour, I managed to take something to reverse the effects, while feeling myself slipping away from this world. But as the next hour unfolded, regret gripped me. The battle raged on, tearing my mind into two opposing forces, two choices, and two enemies. By 4 a.m., I succumbed to the overpowering struggle between the desire to live and the urge to embrace death simultaneously. I took the overdose once more, compounding the danger I posed to myself. By 5 a.m., as the weight of my inner turmoil intensified, I continued down the path of self-destruction.

My mother attempted to wake me, her voice filled with desperation. My sister discovered the evidence of my overdose in the trash, and they both knew the truth. Their screams and shouts, their desperate attempts to rouse me, still haunt me to this day. Though I was only semi-conscious, the words of disappointment lingered on my father's lips, for my actions had not only endangered my life but had also jeopardized our family's very existence. "WE ARE FINISHED," he uttered with a mixture of anger and sorrow. My mother's anguished cries of "WHY" echoed through the room, while my sister read my note, her tears falling in a cascade of heartbreak. Shortly after, they summoned an ambulance. At that moment, I wished I hadn't engaged in that internal war, for then, I would have been dead by the time they discovered me.

This time, my mother accompanied me in the ambulance, while my father chose to stay behind, refusing to join us at the hospital. My sister remained at home with him, burdened by her own pain. She made the call to my fiancé, and he met my mother at the hospital. Deep down, I knew no one would truly comprehend the battle I faced each day. No one would fully understand that my greatest enemy was my own mind. How could I win against myself without losing who I truly was? It was a question that haunted me, gnawing at the depths of my soul.

In that room, with the weight of my actions pressing upon us all, we were bound together by the rawness of our pain and the uncertainty of what lay ahead. The road to healing seemed treacherous, but in the depths of despair, there flickered a fragile flame of hope—a glimmer that perhaps, someday, we could find our way back to the light.

Navigating the Maze of My Existence

At the age of 31, I find myself in a place I never envisioned for myself—unmarried, grappling with mental health issues, juggling TikTok affirmations as a coping mechanism, and struggling with a growing addiction. This is not the life I had planned, nor is it the life I ever imagined.

As children, we are taught to chase after greatness, to set ambitious goals and strive relentlessly to achieve them. But what happens when we fall short? When our dreams remain unfulfilled, and we're left feeling like failures? I've been forced to confront these questions as I navigate through the stormy waters of my existence, peering deep within myself and pondering the very essence of my being. Who am I, and is this the person I truly desire to be? Accepting my current reality has been one of the most challenging hurdles to overcome. Whether it was a result of denial, a lack of mindfulness, or simply being lost in the labyrinth of life, I struggled to come to terms with where I stood. My journey has been filled with losses that preceded any gains, and setbacks that followed those hard-fought victories.

The first time I hit rock bottom, it was a confluence of factors that prevented me from succumbing to the depths of despair. It was a combination of my own inner strength, the unwavering support of those around me, and a flicker of belief that there must be a power greater than myself that I could lean on. In order to understand how my life spiraled out of control, I had to delve into my past and trace the origins of my decline. While the downward spiral began at the tender age of 19, the last 30 years have been marked by significant milestones that have shaped and molded me into the person I am today.

I've come to understand that life is a complex interplay of fate and choice. Some circumstances are beyond our control, dictated by the hand we're dealt or the cards life decides to shuffle. Yet, even within the realm of destiny, we possess the power to shape our own narratives through the choices we make. It is in this delicate dance between fate and choice that I strive to find my footing, seeking solace and growth amidst the chaos.

Today, as I sit in bed, reflecting on the tumultuous path that has led me to this moment, I yearn for a glimmer of hope. I long to rediscover my purpose and forge a new path—one that leads to healing, self-acceptance, and the restoration of my fractured spirit. The road ahead is uncertain, and the scars of my past weigh heavily on my shoulders, but I am determined to uncover the strength within me to rise above the darkness and reclaim my life. For buried within the depths of my soul lies a resilience that refuses to be extinguished—a flame flickering, waiting to be reignited.

The Spark that Ignited the Storm

From late 2017 to early 2019, I ran a small business on the sidelines of my full-time sales job. I made connections with a stranger who claimed that if I financed her business, I could make a profit. I told friends about it, who in turn told their friends, and the business worked like magic for about a year and a half. The money grew, and so did the profit, until I decided to move back to my hometown and cash out.

In early 2019, I discovered that I was a victim of a Ponzi scheme worth hundreds of thousands. My world fell apart, and my friends quickly turned into enemies. Our benefactor had vanished without a trace. I realized that every bit of information I thought I knew about her was fake. The way I was asked to give her cash via the casino was not a way to reduce my tax, but rather a way to safeguard her and the transactions. All the investors, including myself, were around 27 years old at the time, and none of us had done the proper background checks. When one person had asked me for her information before investing, I had given a fake name because I also tried to protect my interests in the business as the middleman who could be cut out at any time. However, it didn't matter because they didn't verify the details given. These silly mistakes led to my downfall. I had people after me because I was the only tie they had to the Ponzi scheme. Over the next year, cases were opened against me, and Facebook posts with my picture were circulated. I had never done anything wrong in my entire life, and this broke me. All the good I had done in life was washed away in a matter of moments.

I survived, but just barely. I tried to make things right by offering my new enemies a payment plan, but it was no use. We were looking at a staggering sum of roughly 650 000 dollars in capital alone, with no profits included - and these people wanted their profits. It felt like a nightmare, a horror movie of my own making. Even worse, my own family's money had been taken. The weight of it all was crushing. It was the first time I truly contemplated giving up.

Thankfully, my fiancé (who was my boyfriend at the time) saved me from myself. He stopped me from downing pills (my first ever thought of killing myself) and took me home to explain everything to my parents. My dad was livid, and my mother was frantic. I could feel their disappointment and despair, and it only made my guilt and shame worse.

For the next few months, I lived with constant fear and anxiety. I couldn't take it anymore. I started gambling, thinking it could be the solution to all my problems - a way to make quick money and pay everyone back, once and for all. I was used to being in the casino, having met the woman who had scammed me there countless times to give her cash. I had even gambled with extra money from her, just for fun. But this time, it was different. This time, I had to make hundreds of thousands from nothing. I needed it all to stop - to stop the legal battles, to stop the disappointment in my parents' eyes, to stop hating myself.

Thus, in July 2020, I started down a dark path towards addiction. I became the same kind of woman who had once stolen from me. As I borrowed more money from people, promising to pay them back with profit, my debt grew higher and my addiction grew stronger. I even took money from my family's banking, trying to replace it by borrowing from outside sources. I knew it was wrong, but I felt like I had no other choice. I was desperate.

Within the labyrinth of my mind, I navigated a treacherous maze of triggers and temptations. Each spin at a slot machine was a desperate bid for a reprieve from my anguish, an opportunity to rewrite the narrative of my life. The momentary flashes of triumph fueled my hope, while the crushing defeats further plunged me into the abyss. I had become a mere puppet, dancing to the whims of chance, my identity stripped away, buried beneath the weight of my addiction. This led to my first official attempt at suicide in November of 2021.

I stayed in the hospital for a week, feeling the weight of my secret overdose hidden from the doctors. Being in the medical field, I knew just how to avoid detection. Only my family of three and my fiancé knew the truth. I had become an expert at presenting myself as the ideal person, concealing the inner turmoil I faced. When I finally came clean to my family, I hoped it would be the first step towards healing. But the addiction was strong and I found myself struggling to repay the small amounts I had borrowed from new creditors while in the hospital. Although these amounts were relatively small, I still felt guilty and anxious about the delays in repayment. And then there was the final creditor, someone who was still unaware of my situation and willing to lend me more money. I saw this as a chance to make things right and try to be perfect again. So, I took more money and went back to gambling, hoping to turn things around. This creditor wasn't expecting repayment until February 2022, giving me time to try and make a profit. He even offered to give me more money, with the promise of even greater pay-outs later on. But it seemed that the universe had a twisted sense of humor. When I had gambled for fun, I had won. But now, when I was desperate, I found myself losing more than ever.

Choosing the Path of Healing

With debts piling up, legal cases rising, and disappointment in myself growing, I had reached my breaking point. In my desperation, I took even more money from my family's account and lost everything once again. In April 2022, I attempted suicide for the second time. I can only imagine how my parents must have felt, the disappointment and despair reaching new heights. In their eyes, I had lost their money in a Ponzi scheme. And as I struggled to come to terms with my failures, I took more money from their account and lost it again. This final blow made them feel as though they had lost everything.

Despite my attempts to end my life, I couldn't escape the overwhelming burden of my problems. Desperately, I prayed for guidance from a higher power, any power that could help me out of this mess. While recovering in the hospital, I knew that I needed to seek help. I couldn't continue living like this, nor could I bear to put my family through it any longer. I searched online for a mental health facility and found a medical centre. I made a call and was put on their waiting list. I planned to go there as soon as I was released from the hospital, after I had figured out what to do legally and with my family.

After two long weeks in the hospital, I was finally discharged and stayed with my fiancé for a few days. My family came to take me home, and thankfully my father had calmed down thanks to the intervention of my sister and mother. To delay settling my debts, I fabricated a story about my money being held up due to taxes and promised to pay all my creditors back on a payment plan borrowed from my father. Although my father was hesitant to forgive me again, he ultimately agreed to help me out financially, and my creditors reluctantly accepted my proposal.

With my immediate problems temporarily resolved, I knew that I still needed help. My family didn't understand the severity of my situation and didn't want me to book into the medical center. Coming from an old school, traditional family, mental health was not seen as an actual issue. I was determined to get the help I needed. I managed to book my first stay within the next two weeks after my discharge from hospital.

Within the Psych Ward: Unveiling the Unseen

In May 2022, I checked myself into the medical facility and stayed there for three weeks. I was incredibly nervous about what it would be like. Would it be like the movies, with wild eyed people swaying back and forth, and pills being pushed down their throats? Or would it feel like a prison? The pictures online showed a peaceful setting, but I couldn't help but wonder if it was all just a facade. Despite my apprehension, I knew I needed the help, and I was ready for whatever they could offer me.

As my fiancé, Vihaan, left me and drove away, a flood of emotions came over me. I felt sad and scared, but at the same time, I felt strangely free. I felt safe knowing that the people who were after me couldn't get to me there. I also knew that the voices inside my head would be under control. For the first time in a long time, I felt like I was in a place where nobody knew me or would judge me based on my specific problems.

There were rules in place:

- Breakfast and pills at 8am

- Classes from 8:30am – 3pm with breaks in between

- Supper at 5pm

- Snack and meds at 8pm

- Bedtime at 10pm

- Phones were allowed between 7-8am and 3:30-10pm

- Make your own beds

- In your spare time: watch TV, play games, do puzzles, read, create art or do nothing

Even with the strict rules in place, the medical facility felt like the most peaceful place in the world. I couldn't forget my problems, but I could deal with them calmly. I felt lucky to have access to this site. Compared to the horror stories I had heard from other patients about their experiences in other facilities, our space was nothing short of a haven. Surprisingly, everyone was "normal". These were high functioning members of society who simply couldn't cope with life and all that it had to offer. The rooms filled mainly with people pleasers who never put themselves first in life.

I was able to have one-on-one sessions with my psychologist and psychiatrist three times a week. Since I had always been good at my studies, I found the group therapy sessions during the day fascinating. Here we learned from psychologists about how the brain worked. After the first week, I fell into a routine. I became familiar with the nurses and had great roommates (two, due to Covid times and one had to leave early after testing positive). By week 2, I started waking up early to go for a 30-minute run on the treadmill. I stayed after class to finish my notes and really take it all in. I started painting rocks and quickly progressed from beginner to intermediate level. I made sure to eat on time and only had coffee once a day. I was prescribed antidepressants and was trying out a sleeping tablet, although I found that I slept well without it. I followed all the rules and it felt right. It felt like I could handle this life...right?

Unmasking the Layers of My Truth

Initially, I felt like a monster, consumed by my addiction and unable to control my emotions. But as I began to uncover the traumas hidden beneath the surface, I realized that I was not a bad person, but rather a victim of my past. Trauma had many faces, and it had been lurking in the shadows of my mind, dictating my every move without my knowledge.

My first few sessions with the psychiatrist and psychologist were overwhelming. I was filled with so much pain and emotion that I could hardly speak without breaking down into tears. But with their help, I slowly began to unravel the tangled mess of my mind and confront the demons that had been haunting me for so long.

My first diagnosis was immediately clinical depression. My other characteristics were hard for me to understand. I could love someone intensely and in the next moment hate them just as intensely and want to live alone. I had no control over my emotions. I had this gambling addiction which helped me avoid the feelings. I was suicidal. I could not take criticism on any matter, without being deeply offended. When it came to any problem, I had to play it over and over in my head and make sure I could solve it, or it would make me feel incomplete. It didn't make sense. I was so good at my job and people praised me all the time for the way I handled situations and stress, but in my personal intimate life I was the opposite.

Antidepressants were given to me, to help my emotions catch up with my mind. It wasn't easy. I had to confront my darkest memories and relive the pain that I had buried deep inside. But with each session, I felt a weight lifting off my shoulders. The antidepressants helped to stabilize my emotions, and I began to see the world in a new light.

The second session with my psychologist, started at the very beginning of my childhood. I didn't have the best or the worst childhood experience, but if I put a cherry on top, you could disguise it as a cupcake. Growing up in what I now know was a dysfunctional household, I had witnessed my parents' constant fighting and my mother's mistreatment at the hands of my paternal grandmother (Aaji). But amidst the chaos, I had found solace in my maternal granny's (Nani) loving embrace.

I grew up for the first five years of my life with my Nani. Looking back, this was the best 5 years of my life. My Nani was nothing short of an angel. Quiet, humble and loving. When I grew up with my Nani, mum (and sometimes dad) would visit on weekends. The one good memory I have of childhood is my parents buying me roller skates and holding my hands on either sides, while running down a parking lot with smiles on all our faces. The other one of me dancing naked on the bed and my Nani saying, "Chi Chi" which is the Hindi version of saying I'm being dirty, but in the sweetest way.

As the days and sessions progressed, I was diagnosed with High-Functioning BPD (Borderline Personality Disorder) and found out it had roots in childhood trauma. Looking back, I realized that my childhood had not been a bed of roses. In fact, it had been far from it. But with the help of my therapist, I began to understand how those experiences had shaped me into the person I had become. As I learned to confront my past and accept my flaws, I found a newfound sense of empathy and compassion for myself.

When Childhood Shadows Shape a Life

As I delved into what trauma could have meant to little me, my heart ached as I recalled the constant battles my mother endured throughout her life. Even as a kid, I remember the pain in my mother's eyes as she faced criticism and scolding from her in-laws. It was heartbreaking to watch her struggle to find acceptance in a world that judged her harshly for a slightly darker skin tone. Growing up, my mother's life was a never-ending cycle of cooking, cleaning, and taking care of everyone around her. Her in-laws never appreciated her hard work, but instead, they made her feel like she was nothing more than a servant. She had to endure the verbal abuse of her husband, a hot-headed policeman, who would often let her deal with his family alone.

As I poured my heart out to my therapist, I found myself defending my mother, who had been through so much in her life. She had experienced unimaginable trauma long before I was born, and yet she still managed to hold her head high and soldier on. I couldn't help but admire her strength and resilience.

These good memories of my mother were short-lived. I started recalling moments of anxiety that came with her presence. I vividly remember my mother's visits to my Nani's house, where instead of greeting us with open arms, she would launch into a tirade about everything that was wrong. It was as though she couldn't help but pick on every little detail, from the way they were dressed to the one dirty dish in the sink. I was just a child, but even I could sense the tension in the air. The house was already crowded with four adults, myself, and my cousin who had a learning disability. It wasn't easy for any of them, but my mother seemed to make it a point to show everyone their flaws.

At the age of 6, I moved back home and went to school near my mum's place of work. Despite the constant battles she faced, my mother always made sure I had everything I needed. She attended all of my school events and forced my father to do the same, even though he was never interested in my life. She went to parent-teacher meetings and I was always the teacher's pet, so it was always great to hear that I was loved by all and my work was outstanding. With the good, also came the bad. Somehow, I was always late for school and every morning was a shouting match to get into the car. After school I went to the library, my cousins' house or to mum's place of work. Here I learned that my mum's main form of talking was shouting. Managing a liquor store meant dealing with rowdy drunk customers, but also sober decent workers, yet no one was spared when she was upset.

She had gone through a lot until her mother-in-law died. I was seven at the time and my sister was just born a few months prior. Similar to me, my sister never grew up at home. Her childhood days were spent at my cousin's house while mum was at work.

At 13, when I moved schools for high school, my mum made it clear that my success was to be my top priority. There would be days when I was running late and she or my dad would often drive me to catch the bus en route to school, but it always came with a lecture about how I needed to get my act together. In the last years of school, my parents spent extra money on extra tuition so that I could get the highest grades. While I appreciated their efforts, I always felt like I had to repay them by being the perfect child in every aspect of my life.

In high school, I treasured my relationship with my mother. I confided in her and shared every little detail of my day with her. She was my rock, my best friend. But things would take a turn for the worse in an instant. A small disagreement about housework could turn into a vicious attack on my character, using everything I ever confided in her against me. I would be accused of being like my friends, of not caring about anything except school, and that my accomplishments meant nothing if I couldn't even do simple tasks at home.

The expectations set on me extended beyond my academics. I am naturally a people's person and love spending time with friends and family. However, the realization of visitors coming over filled me with dread. The night before, we would go over a list of tasks that had to be completed before the guests arrived, including cleaning, cooking, and other activities. If I made even a small mistake, my mother would lash out, criticizing my every move and asking me to do it differently. It seemed like no task was ever done right in her eyes, and her definition of "right" changed constantly. It was as if I could never live up to her standards, no matter how hard I tried. The day of the visit was always the worst. If I woke up even a minute late, my mother's mood would already be tense. I had to go straight into cleaning, not even taking a break to eat, for fear of angering her further. The pressure was immense, and I always felt like I was walking on eggshells. No matter how hard I tried to please her, there was always an argument before guests arrived, and I would end up crying in my room. But when the guests finally came, I had to put on a smile and act like everything was fine. It was like being a robot, going through the motions of hospitality without any real feeling behind it. After the guests left, I was exhausted, but I knew I couldn't rest. My mother expected me to start cleaning up again right away, and if I didn't take the initiative, she would get frustrated. Even now, at 31 years old, I still find myself automatically cleaning up after guests without taking a break to relax first.

Looking back, I realize now that my mother was struggling with her own issues. But as a child, I couldn't understand it. It left me feeling anxious and afraid, like I could never do anything right. Those memories may seem insignificant to an outsider, but to me, they were a formative part of my childhood. They taught me that I was never good enough and that I could never measure up to my mother's expectations.

My sister went through a similar experience, but she quickly learned to set boundaries and keep her thoughts to herself. She eventually distanced herself from our mother, but not before the damage had been done. Even now, my sister suffers from anxiety and panic attacks and has to see a psychologist. It's hard not to consider that our mother's constant criticism and lack of support played a part in her struggles. It breaks my heart to see the impact it has had on her, and it's a constant reminder of the toll that our upbringing has taken on us.

The Haunting Persistence of Trauma

I knew that I was shackled by the suffocating grip of my narcissistic mother. From the moment I took my first breath, I became an unwitting target of my mother's incessant need for validation and control. Her love was a mirage, crafted to manipulate and exploit my vulnerability. Every achievement was belittled, every success overshadowed by her insatiable hunger for attention. Struggling to find my voice in the shadow of a narcissistic monster, I yearned for freedom, for a chance to break free from the emotional chains that bound me to a toxic existence. So in 2010, when the opportunity presented itself, I packed up my bags and left for university.

My mother never cared for our distant relationship. She longed for the idyllic bond she had imagined in her head, one that was filled with happy memories and warm affection. But those memories were selective - she conveniently forgot the times when her words and actions had hurt me deeply.

When I returned home for brief visits from university, I tried my best to connect with my family, to find some common ground that could help bridge the emotional distance between us. But my mother's sharp tongue and sarcastic comments made it nearly impossible. She would belittle me for taking a break from my studies, calling me lazy and ungrateful for the opportunities I had been given. She even accused me of being too smart for my own good, as if my education was a source of shame. I tried to explain myself, to make her see the hurt that her words caused me, but it was like talking to a brick wall. She refused to listen and refused to see the pain that she was inflicting on her own child.

It's painful to think that I was made to feel guilty for wanting a better life for myself. I had dreams and aspirations beyond being just a housewife, but my mother seemed to view my ambition as a personal attack on her. It's hard to believe that a mother would want to hold her own child back from reaching their full potential, but that was the reality I faced.

Looking back, I can't help but feel sorry for my mother. She was so consumed by her own insecurities and regrets that she couldn't see the damage she was causing to her own children. I wish things had been different, that she had been able to appreciate us for who we were, rather than trying to meld us into her idea of the perfect child.

In my first year of university, I fell in love with Aarav, a kind, intelligent man who reminded me of my father. However, our relationship faced a significant hurdle - he was Christian, and I was Hindu. Despite my parents' initial support, I couldn't help but wonder if they were secretly disappointed.

As Aarav pursued his studies, which was funded via a bursary through the airforce, he faced a sudden setback in his third year, failing for the first time. It was a devastating blow, and he failed again soon after, resulting in his exclusion from the program. 4 years later, at the end of 2013, I had graduated and was offered a job as a lab technician. It was a financially challenging time for us, and we had to rely on my parents' help to start a new home. They generously provided us with the essentials we needed, including a spare car from back home. But our happiness was short-lived. The air force requested Aarav to move to a different province and because he was not studying via them, he had to decide whether to continue working or not. If he moved, he would never complete his studies, but if he stayed, we would need to find a way to pay for his education. Our families rallied to support us, but my mother couldn't resist reminding me of my financial dependence on them. Despite their kindness towards Aarav, my mother's biting comments left me feeling like a disappointment and a failure.

As the years wore on, my relationship with Aarav became unremarkable at best. But then, fate intervened in the form of two old friends who were moving to the same area as us. Mira and Serena, my high school classmates, had known Aarav from our early university days. While Mira had initially struggled with her studies and returned home, she eventually found work as a car rental agent at the airport. Meanwhile, Serena had completed her degree but struggled to find work in the area. With housing costs soaring, we decided to pool our resources and rent a cozy two-bedroom house in 2017, splitting the rent between Mira and myself. Unfortunately, Aarav continued to flounder, failing his university courses from 2015-2017 and unable to find steady work. It wasn't until 2017 that he managed to scrape together some employment, working part-time at a courier service company.

But then, things began to take a turn for the better. In 2018, Serena finally landed a job, offering a glimmer of hope for our tight-knit group. My sister was also moving up to start university, so we decided to rent a larger, four-bedroom house together, embarking on a new chapter of our lives.

Amidst the challenges, I never faltered in my commitment to those I cared about. Every morning, I woke up before dawn and drove Aarav to work. Then, I would drive back home and pick up Serena and my sister, dropping them off in the opposite direction before finally heading to my own job. It was a lot to juggle, but I was determined to do it because their happiness and success mattered to me. When we moved into our new, four-bedroom home, it was a relief to have a bit more space. Mira even went above and beyond, securing a job for Aarav at the car rental agency where she worked. It was like our little family had come full circle. We joked that Aarav and I were the parents, while Serena, Mira, and my sister were the kids. But there was truth in the humor: we were all there for each other, providing support and encouragement every step of the way.

After 8 years of dating, in July of 2018, I finally took the leap to end my stagnant relationship with Aarav. It wasn't an easy decision, but I hoped it would serve as a wake-up call for him to start taking responsibility for his life. I needed some space and time to clear my head, so I retreated to my family home for a month. Little did I know that my closest friends had a different plan in mind. They schemed behind my back, encouraging Aarav to move on and setting him up on Tinder, all while leading me to believe that reconciliation was possible. Luckily my sister was still at our apartment and heard everything that was going on.

When I returned, Aarav and I decided to take a trip 3 hours away, hoping to have a heart-to-heart conversation about our future. As soon as we arrived, he left the car to check if the attraction at the site was open, leaving his phone behind. That's when I saw the messages from other girls, and my heart sank. Aarav had been leading me on, pretending to work on our relationship, all while actively seeking out other romantic prospects. When I confronted him, he finally came clean and admitted that he didn't love me.

My world was shattered, and the pain was unbearable. I called my parents, sobbing uncontrollably, seeking solace and comfort. Their response was unexpected, and it cut deep. "We never really liked him. He was holding you back, and he has no direction in life." Their words felt like a betrayal, and it was hard to reconcile the fact that they had kept their true feelings hidden from me for so long. While I knew there was some truth to their words, it was difficult to accept that they had never shared their concerns directly with me before. As a mother, my mum could have chosen a better way to convey her message, and her timing couldn't have been worse.

Matters were not over as easily as I had hoped. The shared house had become a hostile environment, and I felt like an outsider in my own home. Every time I entered the room, Mira, Serena, and Aarav would stop their whispered conversations and cast furtive glances in my direction. Their actions made me feel like they were plotting something behind my back, and it was a constant source of anxiety for me.

As time passed, my suspicions about Aarav and Mira grew. I could feel their bond growing stronger, and I tried to dismiss it as paranoia. But one night, I caught Aarav sneaking out of Mira's room, and the realization hit me like a ton of bricks. One of my best friends and an 8 year long ex-boyfriend were betraying me in the worst possible way. The pain was unbearable, and I cried myself to sleep that night, feeling completely alone and abandoned. I prayed to God, wondering why everything was getting so hard and why Aarav was being so cruel. It was devastating to watch my friends and ex-boyfriend lie to my face and try to hide the affair. I even confronted them, but all I got was denial and anger that I could even mention such a thing.

Eventually, I knew I had to leave. In October 2018, my sister and I got a place of our own, and I started to rebuild my life. However, even as I was leaving, my mother couldn't help but criticize me. "I warned you about your so-called friends," she said. The tension between us only made me feel more isolated and alone.

A few months later, Mira and Aarav announced their relationship on Facebook and jumping to 2022, I found out that they got engaged. The news hit me like a ton of bricks, and I couldn't help but feel hurt and betrayed all over again. The fact that two people, who once pretended to be a father and daughter, are now in a romantic relationship is a strange and unexpected turn of events. The pain of betrayal can cut deep, leaving scars that last a lifetime.

Sometimes, in the midst of our darkest moments, we find unexpected blessings that make it all worth it. And that's exactly what happened to me. When my closest friends and ex-boyfriend broke my heart, I thought I'd never be able to trust anyone again. But fate had other plans. Through a chance encounter with an old friend on Facebook that I had known since I was 6 years old, I found the love I had been searching for all along. Vihaan was everything I had ever wanted in a partner - kind, loving, and supportive. Even though we were separated by distance, we started dating in September 2018 and our feelings only grew stronger with each passing day.

Then, the universe aligned in the most perfect way. 3 months later, I was offered a better job back in my hometown, which meant that Vihaan and I could finally be together. A few months later, news of the Ponzi Scheme broke out and Vihaan stuck by me through it all. It was in the most magical place on Earth in Disneyland Paris, one and a half years later, that he asked me to marry him. I was on a work trip and he flew up to meet me for a few days of vacation. As I said yes, my heart was filled with joy and gratitude. I knew that all the pain I had experienced before had led me to this moment - to the love of my life and the beginning of a new chapter. Even though life can be unpredictable and challenging, I have faith that as long as I have Vihaan by my side, everything will be okay.

A Mother's Legacy: Unraveling the impact

As I delved deeper into my past with my therapist, I couldn't help but feel a wave of sympathy for my younger self. The wounds inflicted by my mother ran deep, leaving me feeling small and insignificant. The way she manipulated and guilt-tripped me, made me feel like I was the cause of all her pain and suffering. It's hard to explain to others just how much her words and actions affected me. The way she clung to her pain and refused to let go, was like a poison that seeped into every part of my life. I became afraid of expressing myself, always worried that I would upset her and trigger another outburst.

For years, I had made excuses for my mother's actions, attributing them to her difficult past. However, I came to realize that my mother was not the helpless victim I had always believed her to be. This was a difficult realization to accept, as it challenged my long-held beliefs and forced me to confront the impact of her behavior on my life and that of my sisters.

Despite having experienced significant trauma in her life, my mother had become stuck in a victim mentality that had a profound negative impact on our family. Even years after the death of her perpetrator, she continued to dwell on her past and used it as an excuse for her behavior. This realization was painful, but it was also empowering, as it allowed me to break free from the cycle of blame and take responsibility for my own healing and growth.

It was eye-opening to discover that my life had been shaped by what is known as ***The Drama Triangle***. I realized that my mother had played different roles in the triangle throughout our relationship. When I was younger, she portrayed herself as the victim, but as I grew older, she became the persecutor. Thereafter, when I faced challenges in life, she would assume the role of rescuer to mask her abusive behavior.

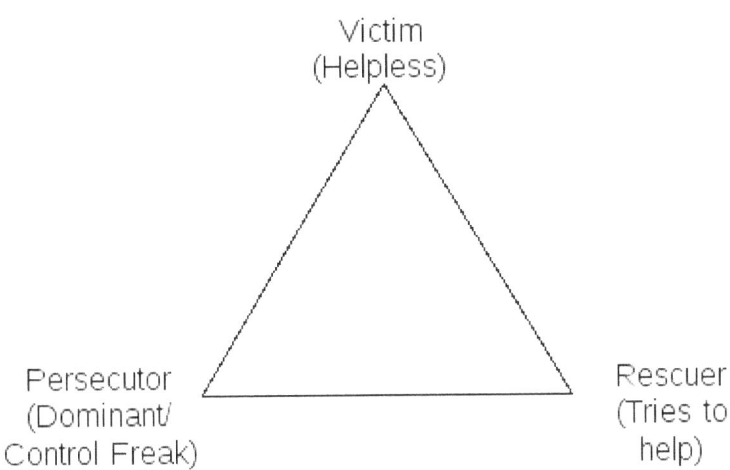

Breaking free from The Drama Triangle was not easy, but it was necessary for me to become emotionally stronger. I had to focus on understanding my own emotions and taking responsibility for my own actions. It was a difficult journey, but with therapy and support from loved ones, I was on my way to gain the confidence and independence I needed to break away from the destructive cycle.

Even now, as an adult, the effects of her emotional abuse linger. It's a constant battle to remind myself that I am worthy of love and respect, despite what she may say or think. I try to remind myself that my mother's own trauma from 23 years ago is likely what fuels her behavior, but it's difficult to feel compassion for someone who refuses to acknowledge the damage they're causing. I've tried countless times to reason with her, to get her to see the error of her ways, but it's a complete waste of time and effort.

My whole life has been a constant battle to be the perfect daughter, but the truth is, I am so far from it. Despite my efforts to be a good person in every other aspect of my life, I can't help but feel a sense of overwhelming disappointment in myself for my inability to manage my finances. I donate to the poor, I treat all people with respect, I take care of the elderly whenever I'm around them, I am an overachiever at work, I make people feel welcomed, I help whenever someone asks for help, I pray for the world and even for strangers on the road who may be struggling. Yet, when it comes to money, I repeatedly make poor choices. I borrow money from others, promising to repay but rarely do. I lie about my financial situation to hide my incompetence, I gamble with my income, and I hurt people's financial wellbeing, all in the misguided hope of fixing the first problem that was ever created. It's a vicious cycle that I can't seem to break, and it fills me with an overwhelming sense of disappointment and self-loathing.

Despite my best intentions, I am a failure in this aspect of my life. It's like I am drowning in a sea of debt, and every time I reach for a lifeline, I end up pulling others down with me. The guilt and shame of my actions weigh heavily on my heart, and I can't help but wonder if I will ever be able to change.

After undergoing therapy, I realized that I had a tendency to view the world and myself in absolutes - either completely good or completely bad. This made me especially vulnerable to my mother's subtle, yet biting comments, which always had a hidden agenda. She would say things like, "We love you, honey, and your happiness is more important than anything else, but we'll have to start over now and we're so old," which sounded like a kind and supportive statement. However, the underlying message was that I was responsible for their financial ruin in their old age. While this was true, she only brought it up to make me feel guilty and trapped. Likewise, she would compliment me for having a supportive partner, only to follow it up with a subtle insult, implying that I was lucky he put up with me when no one else would. Even compliments about my appearance were veiled with criticism, such as, "You have a nice figure, but you could stand to lose a few kilos." The impact of her constant weight-related comments was particularly insidious, and I didn't realize the extent of it until I began therapy. I found myself constantly trying to hide my stomach with a pillow whenever I sat down. I wasn't overweight, but these words had taken root deep in my subconscious, and I had developed a distorted view of my own body as a result. If she couldn't come up with her own criticisms, she would attempt to guilt-trip me by insinuating that my father was unhappy with me. She would say things like, "Why don't you go check on your father? He gets upset when he sees us resting all the time," or "I worry about your father because he doesn't talk about his feelings, but I can see how much it's affecting him."

My sister and I were expected to be the perfect poster children for our family to function. We were adored by other families, both young and old. Our mother would often boast about our helpfulness, our compliant nature when it came to food, our outstanding grades, and numerous extracurricular activities, and how well-liked we were by everyone we met. In hindsight, I believe that my mother's intense desire for us to be seen as perfect may have been driven by the rejection she experienced from my Aaji. Perhaps she wanted to prove that her children were deserving of love and acceptance, even if it meant putting immense pressure on us to always perform at our best.

Revealing the Depths of Psychology

In the journey of self-discovery and healing, identifying emotional patterns is crucial. For me, recognizing the emotional chain of being triggered by my mother's behavior, feeling intense sadness and anger, and then gambling to numb those feelings was a significant breakthrough. I learned that I had been operating on autopilot, which only led to more consequences, triggering me even further and trapping me in a never-ending cycle of depression. It became clear that to break free from this cycle, I needed to stop allowing anyone to trigger me and learn to be in control of my emotions.

Understanding Depression meant I may have a chance to manage my depression and avoid self-destructive behaviors like gambling. I had to learn to recognize when I was having a depressive episode. Depression comes with a range of symptoms, including physical, cognitive, and emotional symptoms. For me, this meant losing interest in most activities, feeling moody, being fatigued, and experiencing negative thoughts, including thoughts of death and suicide. Gambling was my addiction, which was a part of my depressive episode.

From a scientific perspective, depression is caused by a brain that does not function optimally, which is often associated with high levels of stress. There are two types of stress levels: acute and chronic.

Acute stress is short-term stress that helps us to respond in a fight-or-flight situation, providing us with the energy we need to protect ourselves in the moment. The body has a normal state, known as the Parasympathetic State, which is responsible for essential processes such as digestion, detoxification, and cell repair. When we experience acute stress, these functions temporarily stop and we enter the Sympathetic state, which is necessary for protection in the moment.

However, if we remain in a state of acute stress for an extended period, we move into chronic stress, which causes chronic systemic inflammation and neuroinflammation in the body. Living with chronic stress has led to chronic systemic inflammation in my body. To prevent this from happening, I needed to implement changes to my routine.

I needed to manage my stress better, exercise regularly (at least 150 minutes per week at moderate intensity), avoid unhealthy foods (such as processed foods, seed oils, refined carbs, and sugar), engage in more positive conversations with loved ones and trusted individuals, improve my sleep routine, and be mindful of environmental toxins, such as constant exposure to detergents or electronic devices.

While implementing these changes takes time and cannot be done all at once, it was essential for me to identify where I could lessen stress and reduce negative effects on my body. Doing so allowed me to avoid a depressive episode as much as possible.

Mindfulness was also a valuable tool for achieving *self awareness*. By being mindful, I was able to become more aware of my thoughts, feelings, bodily sensations, and their interactions with each other.

In addition, I also had to learn how to communicate effectively with those around me. I realized that keeping everything inside and not expressing my needs, wants, and boundaries only made things worse. It was important for me to learn how to communicate assertively, while also being respectful of others. I had to practice expressing myself in a way that was clear, concise, and non-judgmental, while also actively listening to the other person's perspective.

One of the most important aspects was the need to set healthy boundaries with those around me. This meant learning to say "no" when necessary and not feeling guilty about it. It also meant identifying situations and people that were not healthy for me and learning to distance myself from them. Coming from a traditional brown family, this was particularly difficult because boundaries are not allowed, especially if you're the child. As I used social media to better understand my mental health and the tips and tricks needed, I learned that this actually extends to several cultures. It seems many families expect their children to not have boundaries and setting boundaries is seen as a lack of respect.

Ultimately, by understanding myself better, practicing mindfulness, communicating effectively, and setting healthy boundaries, I should be able to develop better self-regulation and management skills, which allow me to avoid falling back into self-destructive behaviors and help me to start creating a happier, healthier life.

As I explored my inner self while at medical center, I wrote myself poems and words of encouragement in my little book and on one occasion, a love letter that went like this;

Dear Ishani,

Your life is precious. Your time is special. There will always be something you have to do. As you make your to do list, remember to make time for you.

When things seem tough and the worst days are upon you, when the triggers click and the emotions are overwhelming, remember to make time for you.

When you're on the go and life seems good again, when the sun shines and your heart smiles, even then, remember to make time for you.

With everything that you give and every person that you please, remember to please yourself.

You do enjoy doing things. You love listening to music. You love watching crime series. You go gaga for romantic comedies. You have a newfound love for art. The smell of the ocean or the colors on the plate when you cook with passion. Remember who you are.

It will never be the perfect time or the perfect place. You will never be able to fix everything.

There will always be problems. Remember how far you've already made it.

You are you and your time is now. Do what you love. Make time for you. Block out the noise. Be gentle on you.

And remember, there is light and you are safe.

Love you.

Sincerely, your inner you.

Coming from a background where those closest to you, make you feel like you are not enough, I found it important to remind myself of all my accomplishments. In my book of self care and discovery, I wrote it down so I could reflect any time I felt unworthy. I had achieved, what I consider, a lot by 31 years of age. It may not be good enough for my parents, but it's good enough for me.

- In primary school I was on the swim team, the school choir, I took ballet and modeling and I was a prefect

- I was an A+ student most of my life with 5 out of 7 distinctions in Matric

- I got my BSc. degree and my Honors in Genetics

- I've experienced adventour: river rafting. abseiling, canopy tours, microlight across the ocean, horse riding, elephant rides, snorkeling in the middle of the ocean in Thailand

- I was successful at every job I had and was always seen as a leader

- I was proposed to in France at DisneyLand, in front of THE Castle

- I've traveled extensively due to work: South Africa (Limpopo, Gauteng, KZN, Western Cape, North West & Eastern Cape), Swaziland, Mozambique (Portuguese Island), Lesotho, Ireland (Dublin), Switzerland (Rapperswil-Jona, Zurich, Engelberg & Lucerne), UK (London, Scotland – Glasgow & Edinburgh), France (Nice & Paris), Thailand (Bangkok & Phuket), Turkey, Monaco

- Noteworthy Concerts/Plays I have seen live: Ed Sheeran, Katy Perry, Westlife, Trevor Noah, Blue Man Group, The Illusionist, Whitney Huston remake, Disney on Ice, Mamma Mia remake, Swan Lake, The Nutcracker, Matilda, Ultra music festival, H20 music festival

In just 3 short weeks, I learned all of these psychological gems which made the biggest difference on my mental health and stability.

Reconciling Reality: Emerging from the Shadows

Therapy was truly transformative for me. I gained a deep understanding of my triggers, especially legal matters and my toxic relationship with my mother. Despite the challenges I still faced, such as ongoing police cases and the fear of imprisonment, I felt a sense of renewal. I was fortunate to have the unwavering support of my fiancé and sister, who helped me to navigate through the difficulties.

Recognizing the "high functioning" aspect of my BPD was a revelation. It allowed me to better understand myself and my coping mechanisms. I could block out the world when I needed to, but I had to work on managing my addiction to gambling, which was linked to my mother's negative influence. Through therapy, I learned how to identify and manage my mother's comments that caused triggers and how it was vital for me to create an emotionally balanced mind, body and soul.

As I came to learn about *The Emotional Chain*, it was a crucial step in my journey of healing and breaking free from the toxic patterns of my relationship with my mother. Viewing the world and myself in black and white terms, and my mothers effect and hold over me through The Drama Triangle, resulted in me feeling overwhelmed by my emotions and struggling to find a healthy balance.

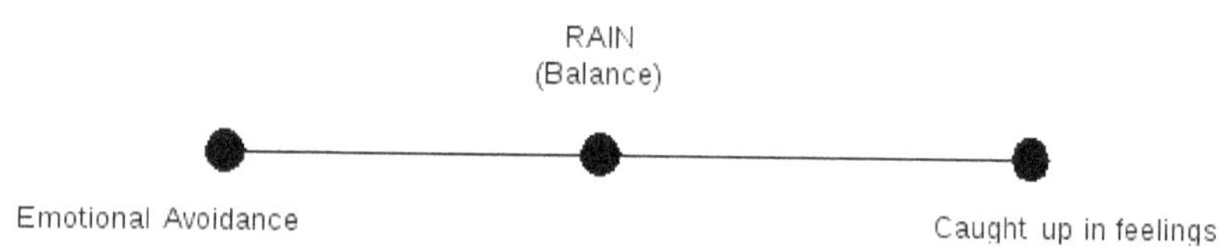

Through therapy, I learned about the concept of emotional avoidance, which is when we try to suppress or ignore our emotions to avoid discomfort or pain. This was a familiar pattern for me, as I had been conditioned to believe that certain emotions were unacceptable or shameful, and that I needed to suppress them in order to be accepted and loved. Emotional Avoidance presented as; using distraction to keep myself busy (social media and TV), looking for an escape (sleeping and my gambling addiction), intellectualisation (over analyzing every situation), somatisation (my emotions always presented themselves with body pains that had no clinical basis) and finally toxic positivity (trying to stay positive all the time as an escape).

On the other hand, I also learned about being caught up in my emotions, which is when I become so overwhelmed by them that they start to control my actions and behaviors. When I was caught up in my feelings, I would do any or all the following; Act out (sulking) or displace my feelings inappropriately (getting frustrated at someone else for no reason) and the all too familiar, ruminating (keep going over the same thoughts).

I needed to learn balance or as the psychologists explained the term, "RAIN".

- **R**ecognize the emotion
- **A**cknowledge and accept the emotion
- **I**nvestigate why that emotion has come up
- **N**urture yourself and find a way to calm the emotions.

If I didn't learn to balance my emotions, I would keep doing the same thing and expecting different results. I needed to know my triggers and how they affected my emotions and actions. I learned techniques to help me find a healthy balance. This included practicing mindfulness, being more self-aware of my emotions, and learning healthy ways to express and process them.

Conducting regular "check-ins" was a helpful practice that I incorporated into my daily routine. I made a point to check in with myself in the morning and before going to bed, dedicating a minute to bring myself into the present moment and find my center. This practice enabled me to cultivate greater self-awareness and enhance my ability to regulate my emotions and behaviors.

From my learning, I put the following method into practice:

- Close my eyes

- Take note of any bodily sensations

- Notice how I feel

- Notice the thoughts that are going on

- Allow myself to feel the emotion freely and don't be critical of it

- Notice the intensity/ energy that the emotion brought with it

- Ask myself what the emotion was telling me about myself or the current situation

- If the emotion was leading me into a stress response, I needed to practice slow belly breathing - Breathe in quick 4 times, pause for 6 counts and let out for 8 counts. Repeat as many as I needed

- Then accept and proceed in the right now/present moment

- Lastly reassure myself and show compassion to myself to make me feel safe

It wasn't easy to break free from my mother's toxic influence, particularly since I still lived at home. But I was determined to put my new tools and coping mechanisms into practice. I started painting, which turned out to be a talent of mine, and I started reading again. I made an effort to exercise daily, eat healthily, and stay hydrated. When my mother made unreasonable demands, I learned to say no and set boundaries. If she got upset, I remained calm and reminded myself to check-in. All of these small steps added up and helped me feel empowered and in control.

I still faced challenges, including financial issues that my parents would sarcastically remind me of from time to time. Sometimes, when I caught a glimpse of myself in the mirror, I could hear her voice in my head, criticizing every flaw and imperfection. And even though I knew that her words were not true, they still had the power to make me feel small and insignificant. I try to remind myself that I am more than just the sum of my flaws, that I am a person worthy of love and acceptance. But it's hard to break free from the conditioning that I've been subjected to for so long. It's like trying to climb out of a deep, dark hole, with only a faint glimmer of light at the top. However, I found solace in speaking with my sister and fiancé regularly and venting any anger or frustrations. Most importantly, I learned that I needed to forgive myself for my past mistakes and take things one day at a time.

A Downward Spiral

As life progressed 2 months down the line, the triggers of my past actions started to take a toll on me once again. My mother would take every positive aspect of my life and turn it into a negative. If I missed a piece of fruit one day, or if it was too cold to exercise on another day, or if I didn't paint or read every single day, she would make sure to comment on it. Even my love for painting wasn't spared. Whenever people came to visit, my paintings were on show for everyone to see and compliment. One on occasion she even asked me to do a painting for a random person's wedding. I explained that they may not like it and may throw it away after all the effort and hours I put in. Her response; "That's fine. At least we gave them something."

Even though I had a full-time job to manage, my mental health to work on, and legal matters to address, it wasn't enough to satisfy them. They didn't comprehend the roles they were playing in my life. Living there meant dealing with the toxic home life. If I had to leave home for my mental wellbeing, they would view it as a sign of my ungratefulness. Furthermore, they believed that because I had stolen money from them, I needed to remain at home to pay them back in chores and be a target for their verbal attacks. Now, don't misunderstand me. I realize that they have to vent because it was also a difficult experience for them. What I did to them was possibly unforgivable. However, how was I ever going to recover and become better if they continued to hold it over my head indefinitely? I didn't do anything intentionally, and I was incredibly apologetic to the point where I wanted to kill myself.

After my discharge, I began traveling frequently for work and spent a lot of time on the road. This enabled me to stay with Vihaan during the week since he lived closer to my workplace, and on weekends, we would split our time between our respective families. Even though my job as an Account Manager required me to travel to labs, my parents didn't consider it a real job because I spent most of my time typing on a laptop. My dad would often make jokes about my job, which was hurtful.

From a religious standpoint, we began observing fasts on Saturdays in honor of Shani, the God of Karma and the ruler of all planets. Initially, I would visit Vihaan's family on Saturdays, and he would visit mine on Sundays. This was because he preferred to cook outside, and my parents enjoyed his cooking on Sundays when we weren't fasting. However, my parents eventually told me that I couldn't visit Vihaan's family on Saturdays because of the meat and alcohol served there. In reality, as long as my mind and heart were pure, my fast would be effective, regardless of my surroundings. They claimed it was against our religious beliefs, but I knew it was just an excuse to keep me at home. As a result, there was a ridiculous expectation to stay at home and pray on Saturdays. However, this rarely happened because my mother often needed my help with shopping or visiting. My parents' disapproval of my visiting Vihaan's family while preserving my fast began to wear on both Vihaan and myself. Soon my parents questioned why Vihaan didn't come over to cook for us, not understanding that we had swapped days due to them. My parents wanted everything to just fall in line around them, because that's what is always expected.

Four months after my discharge, I started to spiral faster. My mother's constant criticism wore me down, and I gradually abandoned my healthy habits. Her words hurt me deeply, and I struggled to cope with my emotions. I tried to talk to my sister and Vihaan about my frustration, but I began to feel like a burden to them. How many times could I complain about my mother before it became tiresome for them? They told me to accept my mother's behavior and move on, but living with her was extremely challenging for me. My medical aid funds had been depleted, so I could no longer afford to see my psychologist. I also started gambling again, which depleted my finances further, leaving me in debt and feeling increasingly suicidal. Despite the decision to attend gambling counseling sessions, I was still caught in the pattern of self destruction. It felt like everything I had worked so hard for was collapsing around me, and I was letting everyone, including myself, down. The sense of hopelessness was overwhelming.

My sister lives in a different town, so in December 2022, she returned home for a three-week visit. During the first week, she worked remotely, and for the next two weeks, she took her annual vacation days. Since she also works on a laptop, her spending a lot of time in her room became a source of conflict. On one occasion, my mother had an argument with her because she felt that my sister was not socializing enough with both of my parents, despite her busy work schedule. My sister would often eat her meals in her room, which further added to the tension. Unfortunately, on one particular day when I was not around, as I was at Vihaan's parents' house, an argument broke out. My heart went out to my poor baby sister, who always held out hope that our mother could change. After that fight, my sister eventually started eating in the living room, but the result was not what she had hoped for. My parents sat there with their phones, not saying a word, so it was all rather pointless.

Slowly but surely, tension began to mount between the women in the household. Regardless of what my sister and I did, my mother would always insist on doing things her way instead. Even when cooking meals we had made countless times before, she would stand beside us and criticize our every move. If we dared to push back, it always resulted in a heated argument because we were perceived as being know-it-all's. Most of the time, my sister and I just gritted our teeth and tried to keep our composure until we could vent our frustrations to each other in private. We had become like robots, just blindly following our mother's every command. If she said to do this, we replied with an obedient "okay." If she told us to do something else, we replied with a placating "sure." When she criticized our efforts, we would ask her how she wanted us to do it, and then simply follow her instructions. It became our mantra: just agree and avoid any potential arguments, no matter what the cost.

On Christmas Eve, I gave my gifts early, because my spa treatment for my parents was scheduled for Christmas day. I bought spa vouchers for myself, Vihaan, my sister and her boyfriend, and my parents. I have a video recording of their reaction, which I wish I could put into this book, to explain how disappointed I felt. My mother appeared as if someone had died, with no hint of a smile. My father stated that he did not like going to spas, which was ironic since he frequently needed a massage from my sister or me, and he had previously enjoyed visiting a spa. The atmosphere was ungrateful and heart-breaking. My sister attempted to cheer them up by urging them to be excited, and then my father responded in his joking dad voice with "Okay, thank you, thank you." My mother muttered a barely audible "thanks." I was devastated and just held back my tears.

On Christmas morning, my sister surprised us with gifts under the tree. She gave me a book I had been wanting to read - Rich Dad, Poor Dad. She also bought my mum a book - The Power of Habits, with the hope that she could make positive changes in her life. Later on, my mother gave me the book, explaining that it was too technical for her to read. However, I suspected that she just didn't want to put in the effort to understand it. My sister had one more gift for our parents: tickets to see UB40 in 2023. They were overjoyed, and my sister and I were happy for them. In this happiness, I couldn't help feeling like I would never measure up to their expectations, because I didn't even get a smile with my gift. In the afternoon, our parents went for their spa day, while my sister's boyfriend's family hosted them for the night. I spent the day at Vihaan's family's house. When they returned, they complained about what they didn't like about their spa day, ultimately saying, "but it was nice." The next day, the remaining four of us had our spa day, and it was fantastic. I knew that this was just how my parents were, and I had no choice, but to accept it.

On New Year's Eve, Vihaan's family invited us to their house and since we had no plans, I was eager to accept the invitation. The thought of spending the evening in a boring and tense environment with my family was not appealing to me. It was a Saturday, and when I told my father about the invitation, he said that he didn't want to go because they would be eating meat and we fast. This statement pushed me over the edge. I told them to do whatever they want and that I was going. Later, my mother came to tell me that my father had agreed to go, but at that point, I didn't care. I didn't understand the need to create drama, when they could have just agreed the first time. In the end, we did go, but when midnight arrived, it was the saddest hug I had ever given my parents at the start of a new year. The embrace felt distant and cold, and I felt like I was breaking apart, piece by piece. I didn't shed any tears because I didn't want to have to explain my emotions to my in-laws. That day, I stayed with Vihaan and only returned home on January 2nd. Vihaan came to stay with me on the 2nd because we had some things to do together on the 3rd.

January 3rd, 2023, also known as the day everything went wrong. The argument that took place at home was beyond words. It was the worst argument one could ever have with a parent, multiplied by seven. The day began with my sister, Vihaan, and me running some errands, and upon returning home, we greeted the domestic worker before walking past our mother who was sitting with her back facing the door. Despite greeting her twice, we received no response. Upon turning back to greet her again, she responded in an arrogant tone, stating that we should have addressed her as "mom" instead of simply saying hello. This set the tone for the argument that was to follow. I couldn't let her attitude go, and my sister told me to just walk away, but my anger only intensified when my mother spoke to me in a passive-aggressive tone when I went to pack some sweets for Vihaan to take away. When I asked her where they were, she responded defensively, leading to a shouting match that escalated quickly. I was so furious that I wanted to slap her, and I even told her that she should have let me die when I attempted suicide. Her response was shockingly indifferent. The argument continued, with my sister crying and begging on her knees for our mother to see what she was doing to us. Vihaan, who normally never says anything out of respect, also intervened. He asked my mother to look inward and think how the fact that both of her children needed counseling couldn't be for no reason. Just by looking at my mother, this short, sweet looking lady, you would never suspect that she could be so vile at her core. She refused to take accountability for her part in the relationship and instead blamed us for treating her badly. By then, I was at my breaking point and my sister and I left to stay at our respective in-laws' houses that night. It was hard to go to someone else's home and pretend to be happy, but we ensured only our partners knew the truth about our home life.

Unfortunately, we had to head back home the next day, because we received the tragic news that our uncle, who was also our neighbor, had suddenly passed away. Despite the tension that still lingered in the air, we found ourselves talking to our mother again, albeit only when necessary. In the background, I was still dealing with new creditors and looming deadlines, while work started picking up again at the beginning of the year. My sister eventually returned to work and left the house, but I couldn't bear to stay with my parents any longer. It had all become too much to handle. I found myself carrying a bottle around with me for two weeks, filled with pills to end my life at any moment. Every day, the temptation to end it all screamed for my attention.

The Urgency of Embracing Help

In mid-January 2023, the suicidal thoughts became too overwhelming for me to bear. I was struggling with stress, anxiety, fear, and felt like I had reached the end of my rope. On top of that, I had dug myself into a deeper hole of debt from gambling and the walls were closing in fast. Despite all of this, I was still working, dealing with my difficult mother, and trying to help my fiancé plan a possible future business. All this and the only thing the outside world saw was a smile.

On 6 January, I had some payments to make to creditors which I fell short of, and they took me under duress to sign an acknowledgment of debt. These creditors worked at the customer that I managed in my role as Account Manager. They took my ID and passport, and it was a terrifying experience. They gave me until 23 January to make a payment, but there was no way I would be able to do it. My attorney asked me not to tell anyone about this, because he knew my mental state was not good and that it would just cause drama for me. I had to keep the whole matter a secret and stay in fear of what these creditors may do next. Slowly, this reinforced that death was the only solution.

On January 18, 2023, the day before my 31st birthday, my fiancé surprised me by taking me for a drive and buying us ice-cream. However, despite his efforts to make me happy, I knew that I was at the end of my rope. The weight of my mounting debts, the stress of work, and the constant turmoil at home had all become too much for me to bear. Two days prior, I had requested to go to the medical center again but was told that there was a two-week waiting list. With everything in my life falling apart, I knew I couldn't wait that long. I started to consider ending my life and made sure to carry my overdose bottle everywhere, ready to use at any moment. However, as I sat with my fiancé on the beach, the war in my head began. Should I tell him about the bottle? I didn't want to burden him with my problems, and I was ashamed of my gambling addiction, which had only added to my debts. Yet I knew if I kept everything inside, I would create unnecessary arguments in an effort to withdraw from meaningful conversation.

I was reminded of one of my first few sessions during therapy about *Creating healthy relationships.* In therapy, we learned about John Gottmann who studied relationships. He spoke of the 4 horsemen and their antidotes. According to him, there are 4 negative behaviors within a relationship that can ruin the relationship, if not handled properly.. I paraphrase them and their antidotes below.

1. Criticism – It's important to talk about the issue and not the person. Do not attack a person's character. Use "I" statements and express your feelings and express a positive need.
2. Defensiveness – Accept responsibility, even for a part of the conflict and don't constantly blame the other person.
3. Contempt – Don't consider yourself superior to the other person. Remove the eye rolls, hostile behavior and sarcasm. Build a relationship based on trust and appreciation.
4. Stonewalling – Practice psychological self-soothing. Don't withdraw from the interaction and stop your mind from drifting.

I was guilty of number 4. I didn't do it intentionally, it just happened because mentally I could not cope. Vihaan was a talker, so he wanted to solve any issue immediately. This was not healthy for us. So, I had to explain and implement the strategies that were taught to me and in this case, it meant;

- Stop the discussion

- Take a 20 min break and stop thinking about the situation (distract yourself)

- Think of positive things about the relationship

- Come together and talk about the issue to get a positive and productive outcome

I also needed to allow myself to become vulnerable with him. Sometimes we are afraid to be vulnerable, because we assume we will be judged, stigmatized or disappointed and even feel like a burden. I just needed to have the courage to put down my guards with those that I trust, so that my healthy relationships could work as a buffer for the toxic ones that I was stuck in.

So eventually, I opened up to him about how much I was struggling but excluded the gambling part. I could not bear to tell this man, who stuck with me through everything, that I was letting him down again. Vihaan is a non-judgmental person. He always makes an effort to comprehend my situation and provide reasonable advice. Although he is unfamiliar with my struggles, he tries his best to be supportive and never intentionally says anything hurtful. He learns from any mistakes and does his utmost to help me. I knew he would support me no matter what, but I was too ashamed to tell him everything. I told him about my suicidal thoughts and the pain of living at home, which he had already witnessed first-hand. Though he didn't want me to leave, he understood that I needed professional help and that he couldn't provide it. He even made me give him the bottle, which he then disposed of.

On my 31st birthday, Vihaan surprised me with a trip to a pottery shop, where we spent the day painting a clay jug and enjoying breakfast. It was a lovely day, and I received some wonderful gifts that made me feel special. Despite everything that was going on in my life, I managed to put on a perfect smile and celebrate the afternoon with my family and in-laws. But on the inside, I was feeling incredibly stressed and anxious, with the weight of my problems bearing down on me.

The following afternoon, I received a call from the medical center asking me to come in on Monday. It felt like a post-birthday miracle. I waited until Sunday night to tell my parents, thinking they would interrogate me if I told them sooner. Their reactions were emotionless; my mother said "That's good," and my father just replied "Okay." On Monday, as I was leaving, my mother's eyes welled up with tears as she showed concern and worry. At that point, I was beyond caring and simply hugged her goodbye. My father left before I did and said his goodbyes while walking away, his back turned towards me as I approached, hoping for a hug. He was in a hurry for work, so I understood. I messaged my sister on WhatsApp and although she was shocked, she remained my cheerleader and was happy for me. My inlaws were under the impression that I was going away for work.

During my second stint at the medical center, was when this book began. All it took was a 4 year old Ponzi Scheme, pending legal matters, a gambling addiction, 2 almost suicide moments, 2 actual suicide attempts and 2 admissions into a psychiatric facility. If not a book at this point, someone could have made a movie.

The Shackles of a Gambling Addiction

Gambling was a seemingly harmless tool I turned to in order to navigate the challenges and debts that weighed heavily on my shoulders. Little did I know that beneath its surface, a complex web of psychological factors was at play, tightening its grip on me with each passing day. I learned that the same is true for any addiction. The brain's reward pathways are hijacked, leading to a cycle of craving, indulgence, and temporary relief, perpetuating the addictive behavior.

At its core, my gambling addiction was driven by a desperate need to escape. It wasn't about the thrill of winning or the chase for rewards; it was a means to temporarily overcome the overwhelming challenges I faced. In the midst of my battle with depression and anxiety, gambling seemed like a way to silence the relentless demons tormenting my mind.

The allure of casinos, lottery tickets, and online gambling provided a fleeting refuge from the harsh realities of life. The dimly lit halls, the sounds of slot machines, and the flickering hope of a life-changing jackpot created a glimmer of solace in a world where everything seemed uncertain. Every dollar I took from others was not spent on enjoyment or personal gain; it was poured straight into gambling as a desperate attempt to find temporary relief from my problems. The pursuit of rewards or wins became secondary; it was the momentary respite that mattered the most.

But as time passed, my supposed escape transformed into a suffocating trap. The grip of gambling addiction eroded my self-esteem and shattered my relationships. The debts piled up, weighing me further down with a sense of hopelessness that seemed insurmountable. What was once a tool to cope became a prison, trapping me in a cycle of despair, regret, and shame. I struggled to reconcile my actions with the person I aspired to be. Trust in my relationships crumbled, pushing me further into isolation and despair.

Breaking free from the clutches of addiction demands immense strength and support. For me it meant confronting my demons head-on, untangling the web of triggers that ensnared me, and seeking professional help. I signed up for gambling counseling a few weeks before my second admission to the medical center. However, my journey to recovery was riddled with obstacles. Gaps between counseling sessions, due to work commitments and other challenges, allowed me to slip back into gambling, hiding the truth out of shame and fear. Similar to my mental health counseling, I was told that gambling counseling was not a magic cure and that it took time and relapses to get over it.

The Emotionally Estranged: Navigating Parental Disconnect

As I started my classes again, I found myself falling back into a routine that I knew worked well for me. I woke up early, exercised, had a refreshing bath, and enjoyed a hearty breakfast before diving into my studies. While there, and in an attempt to pay off the debts I owed, I found myself borrowing new money. I was lost and lived in a lie that a lucky spin could make it all better.

Meeting with my psychiatrist and psychologist again, I opened up about my recent relapses. I couldn't understand why I was struggling again after feeling like I had made so much progress. I knew my mother caused my triggers and I tried to avoid getting caught up with her as much as humanly possible. If I was failing at escaping her taunts, what else could possibly help me? In my mind, I told myself, "You have a problem. You know what's causing it. You are not able to fight it. What more can you possibly learn that will make a difference? Why wasn't it enough the first time around?"

They again prescribed me antidepressants and some new anxiety medication, which I needed more than ever during the second week of classes. It was then that I realized the root of my core troubles: both of my parents. Memories of my childhood resurfaced, and I was filled with anger towards them. For lack of a better word, my childhood sucked. We never spent quality time together as a family, never went out for meals or movies, and never played games together. The only time we ever did anything as a family was during our occasional beach trips, and even then, it wasn't a big deal. Even birthdays were barely celebrated, until my sister and I were old enough to organize them on our own. I began to understand how my parents' lack of attention and affection had affected me. Not that it suffices as an excuse, but it was no wonder I had turned to gambling and self-destructive behavior to fill the void.

As therapy continued, I came to see that I had overlooked the impact of my father in my life. He was a mere spectator to the turbulent and traumatic events that unfolded within our home, choosing instead to immerse himself in his work and leaving us to fend for ourselves. His complete disinterest left a void in my heart, an insatiable yearning for his guidance, warmth, and love that was never satisfied. I still think back and wonder if I would be where I am today, had my father offered to help me financially, when I was first a victim of the Ponzi Scheme.

I recall yearning for a father who would be present, who would listen, care, embrace, inspire, educate, and shield me from the world's cruelty. But my father was never that man. He was merely a stranger, an indistinguishable figure that lingered in the background, a vague silhouette without any real presence in our lives. Witnessing other families with adoring fathers who take an active role in their children's lives only compounds my sadness and envy. Why couldn't I have had a father like that?

Growing up, he was always present but somehow absent at the same time. We never discussed anything related to our personal lives with him. My sister and I never told him when we got our period or asked him to buy pads. As kids, he bought us toy cars instead of dolls. He provided us with everything we needed materially, but he was never interested in connecting with us on an emotional level. He loved mechanical work and would often brush off my attempts to bond over it. If I ever tried to engage him in conversation about it, he would say, "I'm too busy," or "What will you understand?" We never talked about relationships or boys. When I dated Aarav, I waited until graduation 3 years into the relationship, to introduce them. Even after that, my dad had no interest in my personal life.

He never knew the names of our friends, except for maybe one best friend, and he couldn't tell you what we were studying in school or what our interests were. He just saw our results at the end of the school term and would joke with us about losing two marks if we got 98/100. He didn't believe in any special occasions like birthdays or Fathers Day and he never motivated us. When I expressed interest in forensics, his favorite line was always, "You are scared of a lizard. How will you do forensics?" My father had never had an emotional connection with his own parents, and it seemed that he couldn't give it to us either, unless he made a conscious decision to break the cycle. But as I looked back on my childhood, I realized that I had learned to cope with his emotional absence, by trying to be as emotionally attached to my mother as possible.

As I continued looking into my childhood memories, a deep sadness consumed me as I came to further realize just how money-driven my parents were. To them, everything was about saving and making a profit, even if it meant tearing a paper towel in half or not using paper plates if the domestic worker was present. If it meant driving to another shop to save a few bucks, it was worth it. Stocking up on groceries during sales and then using them beyond their expiration date, because apparently that is just a suggestion, was a norm. It was all about the money, and I had been conditioned to think the same way. It was no wonder I fell victim to the Ponzi Scheme in the first place, by trying to make money. But the true extent of my parent's obsession with money hit me like a ton of bricks during a family video call while I was at the medical center. My dad made a feeble attempt at humor, and I responded with a joke about booking him into the facility. His response was callous and uncaring: "No, that place is for mad people. If people want to come right, they must come to me and I will show them hard work and fix them. At the medical center, you sit the whole day to paint one flower." His words stung me deeply. My sister realized the impact and she took offense on my behalf, telling him how negative and hurtful his words were. But our father couldn't understand why his comments were hurtful, as all he cared about was making money. He even went on to say, "You can't make any profit from sitting there and painting one flower. If you work here, at least you can make money." I realized that my parents had always been more concerned with making money than enjoying their lives. It was a deep-seated urge that had followed them their entire lives, and it had now infected me. We were not poor, even though I lost a significant amount of our money in the Ponzi Scheme, but everything always went back to money. I agree that my dad works extremely hard to provide for us, but it was never given freely. We were always made to feel obliged to him for anything we were given.

The worst moment was when I sat on a call with Vihaan and told him how during my second suicide attempt, my fathers words were all about them being finished in regards to their finances. Both my parents hung over me, as I laid there losing life, and could only deal with the realization of losing more of their money. For me, I had thought this was a normal reaction after what I had done, until my therapist said to me, "Ishani, if it were my kid, I would be pissed off and they would hear about it BUT later. First I would worry about them and their life and rushing them to hospital immediately." WOW! Is that what parents are supposed to be like? As I sat to think what I would have done in that situation, it became more apparent that I am surrounded by money issues and people who obsess over money in every aspect of life.

During a group session with psychologists, one of them explained that having an emotionally distant parent is like repeatedly walking into a wall, hurting yourself, gathering hope on your way back, and then walking back into that same wall. This analogy struck a chord with me because it's been my reality since I was six years old, if not earlier.

I now refer to my parents as "Admin Parents" because they fulfilled the basic requirements of providing me with food, shelter, clothing, and an education. I was expected to be grateful for it, despite the childhood trauma, the toxic environment, the lack of validation, and the constant pressure to be perfect. They checked off all the boxes of what parents are supposed to do materialistically, but they were never there for me emotionally.

Many parents fail to acknowledge the existence and the impact of generational trauma and unless someone takes the initiative to break the chain, future generations are likely to be trapped in the same cycle. It's common for some to dismiss the newer generation as overly emotional, but emotions are a fundamental part of being human. Failure to recognize the influence we have on others can limit our ability to make a positive contribution to the world.

As I faced my own mental health challenges, I knew that I needed to confront my past and deal with the emotional baggage that I had carried with me for so long. Armed with the help of my doctors and a newfound understanding of my past, I was determined to break free from the cycle and take control of my future.

Shattering Emotional Chains

The emotional weight of my unraveling situation was almost unbearable. My mother finally called me, 5 days after my admission to the medical center. Her voice was filled with sorrow and regret, as she struggled to express her love for me. I listened to her empty promises of change, knowing that it was just another cycle of disappointment waiting to repeat itself. Her words felt hollow, devoid of any real meaning or intention. I was drained from the endless attempts to connect with her and the lack of progress. Every word spoken felt like an echo in an empty space, an emotional void that could not be filled. On one occasion, she even lied that she was seeing a psychologist. We only found out that this was a lie later on, but it just validated how meaningless her words had become.

During one group therapy session, we delved into the complex emotion of grief. Our therapist asked us to focus on a common feeling that arises during the grieving process - anger. Whether it's the loss of a loved one, an opportunity, or a relationship, anger is often a part of the journey. I closed my eyes, ready to confront the deep-seated anger I harbored towards my mother, and the newer, less intense anger towards my father. But as I looked inward, instead of anger, I felt a flood of sadness and disappointment. I realized that I had been holding on to an illusion of a happy family, ignoring all the wrongs my parents had done throughout my life. As tears streamed down my face, I mourned the loss of my idealized family. It was as if I had witnessed my parents' deaths, and my heart shattered into a million pieces.

All this time, I had been desperately trying to undo the damage of my past mistake, hoping that somehow it would make everything right again. But deep down, I knew that my efforts were futile. It wasn't just about the money anymore. It was about the constant guilt-tripping, the shame, and the never-ending cycle of depression that I found myself in. For years, I had been striving for my parents' approval, hoping that they would finally see me as the successful, responsible adult they wanted me to be. But the truth was that their expectations were impossible to meet. Even if I managed to pay back all the money I owed and close all my cases, it wouldn't change who they were at their core.

I felt a sense of hopelessness wash over me as I came to terms with this harsh reality. The weight of my parents' constant disapproval and emotional manipulation felt heavier than ever before. It was like a dark cloud that hung over me, suffocating me with its never-ending presence. I realized then that the only way to break free from this cycle was to accept that I couldn't change my parents, and that I needed to start living my life for myself, rather than for their approval.

The Abyss of Mental Disconnection

The next few days were a blur. I couldn't escape the feeling that my entire life had been a sham, a facade that I had built to try and make up for the lack of love and attention I received growing up. It's exhausting to even consider delving into any other issues I may have, because they all seem to stem from this one root cause.

I spoke to my psychologist about my detachment and lack of interest in anything, and her concern only made me feel worse. The truth is, I just didn't care anymore. Not about my job, not about my relationships, not even about my own well-being. The idea of ending my life didn't scare me the way it used to, because it seemed like the only way to truly escape the overwhelming sense of emptiness. My therapist noted that my previous suicide attempts weren't about wanting to die. They were about wanting to escape my circumstances. Now, with my emotional detachment, I was at a higher risk of truly wanting to end my life. The thought terrified me, but at the same time, it was hard to muster up the energy to care. I was stuck in a limbo, unable to move forward or backward, just existing in the nothingness.

As I sat there, the thought of leaving in just one week's time terrified me. It had been two weeks since I arrived, and the idea of returning to the outside world, where everything seemed overwhelming and out of control, was almost too much to bear. I could feel myself slipping away, like sand slipping through fingers. The days blurred together, and I couldn't remember the last time I felt genuinely present in the moment. During one of my last sessions with the psychologist, I couldn't find the words to express how I was feeling. It was as if my emotions had shut down completely, leaving me feeling numb and disconnected from everything around me. I was aware that this was a dangerous place to be - that if I didn't snap myself back into reality and start caring again, I could lose myself completely. But it was hard to care when nothing seemed to matter. I found myself drifting off in class, unable to concentrate on anything for more than a few minutes at a time. Even sleeping had become a struggle - I woke up feeling exhausted, as if I'd been running a marathon all night. And then there were the dreams. Dark, twisted visions of violence and chaos, where I was either on the brink of killing my mother or defending her from my father's family. It was all so confusing. I didn't know what was real anymore. Maybe I was losing my mind. The thought of slipping into psychosis scared me more than anything else.

I had to go back home and live with people I didn't recognize anymore. Saying "I love you" to my parents would become a mere obligation, not a genuine expression of affection. They were administrative figures, and the lack of emotions in our lives would become more apparent when I went back home. I held on to the hope that I could marry Vihaan soon and leave that house, but the pending legal cases were also hanging over my head. Marrying him and then ending up in jail also seemed inevitable. So where was my life going? I was just so tired. I just wanted it all to go away. At that moment, if someone could find me a mountain with no people and berries to survive, I would happily live the life of a monk. I just wanted to scream, "STOP! ENOUGH! PLEASE! STOP!"

Finding Respite and Moving Forward

All the psychologists from the center met once a week and discussed their patients with each other. My psychologist told me that she described me like this – Simply put, Ishani's mother has taught her to self loathe. When she told me this, I was confused but intrigued. She said that meant that I would always seek out self-destructive behaviors, because deep down, I have been trained not to like myself. Not to feel good enough. I will always return to do things that will eventually prove that I am not worthy. I was so tired of feeling like my my mother had all the power.

It was time to go back to a house I once considered a home. I need tools or I wouldn't be able to do this. In order to even consider moving on, I needed to learn to forgive. Forgive those that hurt me. Forgive myself and eventually forgive those who continue to hurt me.

Forgiveness is a powerful tool for personal growth, but it's not always easy to achieve. For me, learning to forgive meant understanding what forgiveness is not. It's not about condoning or excusing someone's hurtful behavior, forgetting what happened, denying the situation, or even reconciling with the person. Instead, forgiveness is about taking back our personal power from those who hurt us.

One quote that really resonated with me was, "To forgive is to set a prisoner free and discover that the prisoner was you." This quote by Lewis B. Smedes captured the essence of what I needed to do. I needed to let go of the suffering I was holding onto and forgive those who had hurt me, even if they never acknowledged or apologized for their actions.

However, I also realized that forgiveness is not always possible when you're still in a relationship with someone who's causing you ongoing pain. In those situations, it's important to work through the issues and pain first before considering forgiveness. For me, this meant writing letters to those who were no longer in my life but had hurt me in the past. These letters were for me and helped me accept and forgive those individuals. But with my current relationships, especially my relationship with my parents, I needed to learn how to deal with the pain until I could find a way to break free from it.

One of the other symptoms from my BPD is the ability to fill the unknown with negativity. I created a list – Worst Case Scenarios. I realized whenever I can't cope, comprehend or deal with the unknown, I only think about killing myself. This is because my mind can't comprehend what the worst case looks like in different situations. If I new what the worst case scenarios were and was willing to accept it, nothing could convince me to kill myself. So here it was, for me to accept and to remember in those times so that I could have courage and face life head on.

Situation 1: Legal cases

Worst Case: I go to jail

Solution: I serve my time. I come out and start over. I will not die in jail and I will be in a women-only prison

Situation 2: My job

Worst case: I lose my job

Solution: I look for a new one. I am qualified and can find something

Situation 3: My wedding/relationship

Worst case: Vihaan and I will be separated if I go to jail

Solution: I spoke to him. No matter what, he has decided he will wait for me and does not want to end the relationship

Situation 4: Parents

Worst case: Disown me and don't love me

Solution: For 31 years, my mother and father have had control over my life. I will forever be grateful for the duties they did fulfill, but I don't want to forever feel the lack of duties they didn't fulfill. So if need be, I can walk away too.

Feeling slightly more hopeful, I wrote to my child self;
Little girl, little girl
Things will get better.
Right now you are numb,
But soon emotions will flow.
Like a phoenix, you will rise,
And your life will start again.
Those that hurt you, will no longer control you,
Those that love you, will help you find your way.
You were meant for more,
But you were shackled by others and your own mind.
Let's try again,
Maybe there are second, third or even fourth chances,
For a new life.

Against All Odds: The Unyielding Journey Continues

It has now been about 3 months since I left the medical center. I have completed my gambling counseling and have met virtually with my therapist once.

I have undergone one of my worst-case scenarios. I got dismissed from work. This came after a 3-month suspension and investigation which was initiated by one of the creditors I owe. Remember the ones that took me under duress? Yep, those ones. The charges brought against me - actionable misconduct, deception, moonlighting, abuse of company property, and bringing the company's name into disrepute. All they had were WhatsApp messages to prove that I asked for money for other purposes. I denied all charges at work, but the company found it damning enough. I provided evidence to show they took me under duress. I found loopholes in their affidavits, bringing their character into question and I even mentioned to the third-party chairperson of the hearing, that those WhatsApp messages were faked. The only way they verified it was on the complainant's phone via a video call. They did not even check my own work device to confirm this. Surely that could not be enough to dismiss me after 2 years of exemplary work and a clear record. The chairperson used the social media posts regarding other cases as ammunition to state that I must be guilty and further went on to state that I showed no remorse. How is someone who denies all allegations supposed to show remorse? He also stated I could not be trusted in my senior position. My misdeeds had nothing to do with the company. I gave work my all. It was my safe space, and I was transparent with them about my cases when I was hired. I also told my manager about all my times in the medical center and ensured he knew what was happening. They dismissed me and defamed my reputation based on a third-party complaint and WhatsApp messages that were not even verified by someone in IT. Now the question is do I want to fight the decision? I feel like I have a very strong case. Yet a part of me does not want any more drama. There's a lot of legal talks to have with my lawyer and decide on the best way forward, because I have actual court cases pending that I did not want to put into jeopardy. My lawyer also thinks the best case is a 3 month salary, which considering what I would have to go through, would not be worth it.

I am planning my wedding for August and am hoping I have the money and am around to enjoy it. Planning this wedding is the only thing that kept me sane during my suspension and it is the only glimmer of hope I have left for my future. It means I can leave home and finally get out of the toxic environment. Unluckily yet luckily for me, I had to give my work car back when they dismissed me. That means I don't have my own vehicle, but it also means I can stay with Vihaan and only go to my parents when he is available. A blessing in disguise.

I mentally disowned my mother and just don't care about my father's opinions anymore. I had a huge fallout with my mother which led to this. She really just pushed all the wrong buttons. It was a Saturday afternoon and I was not well. My sister had come down for a long weekend and they had to go to our Guru to do some prayer that she missed out on. When she returned, she sat with me to tell me everything the Guru said. My mother, upon seeing us talking, decided she was bored, I guess. She started shouting, "I am not stupid, I know you are talking about me. I don't need this. You think I was born yesterday." My sister told me to ignore it, but like a devil with a pitchfork, I took a trip to hell. I lost it completely. I called my father. I shouted and swore and cried. I had had enough. I cannot deal with the constant negativity, her empty promises of seeing a psychologist, her poking and probing. My sister and I sat and cried and tried our best to make her see the light... again. This was just another one of those days. It would not affect her, but we would get another dose of trauma. Eventually I went to my sister and in front of both my parents, told her to stop trying. I told her that if our mother was going to change, she would have. If she was going to love us, she would have. If she wanted to fix things, she would try. She just sits there and does this over and over and it's never going to change. My sister started having a mini panic attack and obviously my mother instantly blamed me and my father agreed. My sister also lost her mind and told them to stop blaming me for everything. She said to my mother, "When I disown you, when I don't talk to you or visit, don't tell people I just left. Tell them I tried, and I spoke to you year upon year, and you didn't care. You didn't meet me halfway. You never took accountability." My mother sat there, straight faced and not taking accountability. It's so hard to not feel like crap, even though you know you are looking into the eyes of a narcissist. You want so much to have your own mother try, just try. I think it really demolished me. Yet once again, a few weeks later, she is being all loving because she found out I lost my job. The ever-caring mother who comes with empty promises again of seeing a psychologist. From my drama triangle, I know she is back because she wants to pretend to be my rescuer. No thank you.

Vihaan tries to help me cope by telling me to just tick boxes with my parents. What he means is; make conversation, check-in, pretend. Unfortunately I no longer have the capacity. I am still biased towards my dad, so he gets more conversation from me than my mother. However, I think many people assume it's easier to just avoid the drama and play nice, but the toll it takes when you are directly affected is too great. I pose the question, "If instead of my parents, had it been a man treating me the way my mother does, would anyone ask me to just put up with it?"

When I went to the medical center the first time, I had to kill the image of my loving parents I had made up in my head and that was the toughest session. This time I had to just kill my parents off completely. I don't know what stage follows this, but I can say that I am done caring. They can think whatever they want off me, say whatever they want and do whatever they want. I do have parents, just not of this world and for that I find my solace in Shiv and Shakti – the Hindu source of life. I console myself by thinking that eventually, one day, I will return home to them. They must be protecting me, otherwise how do you explain 2 failed suicide attempts, multiple open cases and no jail time (yet), people who hate and threaten me, but I am still alive and fighting? Someone is definitely watching out for me.

My latest session with my psychologist was a virtual one. We spoke about my mother in general. This was prior to the whole drama. In general, the conversation seemed pointless because we had been over this already. I took her through what was happening at work and my idea to try and get out of it, and she asked me a really good question, "For how long?" What she meant was, for how long am I going to have to keep making up lies? For how long was I going to hide from the open cases? Fair enough I may not go to trial now, but what happens if the other shoe falls only when I have kids? Her suggestion was that maybe it's time I just come clean. Then no one can hold anything against me. I can't be made to feel guilty and be triggered into gambling further. Worst case I go to jail for taking people's money for gambling, I serve my time and I come out and start fresh. That feels doable to me. It feels like peace and calm. I can manage staying away from everyone. Not that I know how jail is, but I like to think that some guardian angel will guide me while I am in there. It is very easy to just want to do that and get it over with, but I don't just ruin my life in the process. I also ruin the reputation of everyone who is dear to me. Vihaan is okay with whatever decision I make. He understands the toll this all takes on me, but like my lawyer, doesn't want me to be silly about it. If I must go to jail, then I should try to get the minimum sentence possible. Yes I did wrong things and must atone, but my intention is and never was to hurt anyone. It's a very tough choice, picking between clearing my conscience and trying to clear my name.

I still roam around with a dream that 1 million dollars may magically appear and help me to just close off every debt and start a new life. A life where I can paint, read, write, help people and just do good. It's such a simple life that I crave, but such a complicated one that I am in.

My mental health therapy and addiction is not going to be magically fixed, it's a journey. I may keep failing, but I won't stop fighting. I hope to help others on my journey of finding myself. What I do know for sure, is that it is my life and the power must lie with me. I struggle daily to get my power back, but that means I am alive.

The hurt that comes from a toxic family dynamic is one that is difficult to put into words, but it is a pain that is shared by so many. I hope that my story can serve as a reminder that you are not alone in your struggles, and that healing, and growth are possible, even in the most difficult of circumstances. I am not sure where the road goes from here, only that I just have to keep trying to become the person I aspire to be. I am slowly moving on from my family and trying to create my own. I just hope the universe can manifest a happy ending for me someday.

THE END (for now)